C000263743

21

THE SIMPLE GUIDE TO
CUSTOMS AND ETIQUETTE
IN
CHINA

COVER ILLUSTRATION

The Great Wall of China is 2150 miles long (3460km) and snakes its way from the coast north-east of Beijing (Peking) to the deserts of inner Mongolia. It was originally built during the Qin Dynasty (221–206 BC). However, most of what exists today was built during the Ming Dynasty (1368–1644).

ABOUT THE AUTHOR

CAROLINE MASON is Lecturer in Chinese Language and Civilization at the University of Durham, England. She has had extensive contact with China during the past twenty years, as well as considerable experience as a translator and interpreter. She is also co-author (with Don Starr) of *Very Simple Chinese*.

ACKNOWLEDGEMENTS

The author wishes to thank her colleagues at the Department of East Asian Studies, University of Durham, for their suggestions and comments on the original draft of this book, and is grateful also for the help received from Katherine Duxbury, Gabrielle Harris and staff at the China-Britain Trade Group.

ILLUSTRATED BY
IRENE SANDERSON

THE SIMPLE GUIDE TO CUSTOMS AND ETIQUETTE IN

CHINA

CAROLINE MASON

GLOBAL BOOKS LTD

Simple Guides • Series 1
CUSTOMS & ETIQUETTE

The Simple Guide to
CUSTOMS & ETIQUETTE IN CHINA
by Caroline Mason

New Edition 1995 by
GLOBAL BOOKS LTD
PO Box 219, Folkestone, Kent, England CT20 3LZ

ISBN 1–86034–030–X

British Library Cataloguing in Publication Data
A CIP catalogue entry for this book
is available from the British Library

Distributed in the USA & Canada by:
The Talman Co. Inc
131 Spring Street
New York, NY 10012
USA

Set in Futura 11 on 12 pt by Bookman, Slough
Printed and bound in Great Britain by
The Cromwell Press, Broughton Gifford, Wiltshire

Contents

Foreword

'China still carries with it a sense of the exotic'

For many people the word 'China' still carries with it a sense of the exotic, of an oriental mystique which tantalizes and fascinates. It can conjure up a picture of straw-hatted coolies, of slender women with tiny bound feet, of gleaming green rice paddies and outlandish cuisine. It often seems to me that Westerners prefer this vision of China to one which is closer to the truth, because it is identifiably 'different' and can be safely pigeon-holed – but, although much of China *is* still at a relatively primitive stage of development compared to the West, the visitor who goes there with such images in his/her head will be in for a great shock.

There have been enormous changes, especially in the People's Republic of China

(PRC) in the past few years, and while Taiwan has already been modernizing at a remarkably fast rate for a long time, mainland China, too, is now in many respects catching up with the West. You will still see steam-trains and abacuses, but you will also see BMWs and computers; you may still spot an old granny with bound feet, but you are more likely to see young women in designer outfits and high heels.

Both the PRC and Taiwan are now much more 'liberal' than they were before, in economic terms certainly but also in political terms, and with this liberalization has come a remarkable increase in wealth. In the PRC, the recent years of 'reform and opening up' have brought about changes which one would think are irreversible – but this is China, where nothing is predictable. There have been great upheavals in the country before, and there may well be again.

C.M. MASON
June '95

Introduction

Temple of Heaven, Beijing

Any first-time visitor to China who reads this guide will find some valuable stepping-stones regarding correct behaviour in many of the commonly-experienced contexts of everyday life. However, the business visitor to China in particular, who may well have already boned up on such matters as Chinese negotiating style, China's recent economic boom and new market openings, could well find here some important insights into more general Chinese customs and etiquette – the 'background', as it were, to doing business. Even a slight knowledge of these aspects of life in the Chinese world will be helpful to someone trying to come to grips with a culture and society which are still, even at the end of the twentieth century, so different from our own.

In traditional China, great importance was attached to correct behaviour within society and one of the earliest classics of Confucianism was a collection of writings on the complex details of what is translated variously as 'ceremonial', 'propriety' or 'the rites'. Today, fortunately, ideas about correct social behaviour are much simpler: they have had to change, as Chinese society has changed, and although attention is still paid to etiquette, and many traditional customs and conventions are still observed, nearly all of these are of the kind with which foreigners can at least attempt to become familiar.

Most of what is said in the following pages applies both to the People's Republic of China (PRC) and Taiwan. Where it applies to one and not the other, I shall make this clear. But it should be borne in mind that since the People's Republic covers a vast area, there are bound to be regional differences in every field, and it is obviously beyond the scope of this book to detail them all.

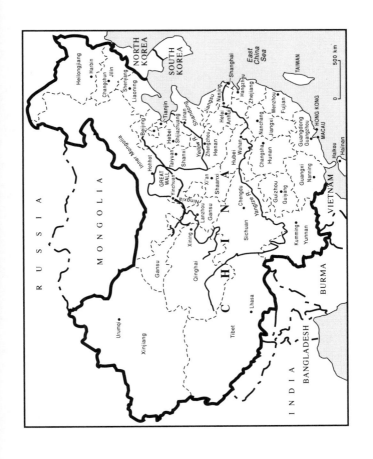

1

The Past

The army of Qin Shi Huangdi 210 BC

Chinese people will frequently tell you, with pride, of their '5000 years of history', but in fact they go back much further than that. Archaeologists have found evidence of Neolithic sites dating from before 5000 BC in several areas of the country, and by the time of the Shang dynasty, which flourished in the middle of the Yellow River valley in the second millennium BC, a very sophisticated culture had developed, with a high level of bronze-manufacturing technology and a written language.

The Shang were replaced by the Zhou, but it was not until the Qin dynasty unified the various feudal states which had grown up in different areas of China that a truly centralized government appeared. Already, however, the idea of 'Chineseness' referred less to geographical frontiers or to racial traits than to cultural differences, and that continues to be the case.

Though based originally on the Han Chinese region of the Yellow River basin, the Chinese empire always included many non-Chinese peoples, as the borders of the Empire expanded and contracted at different times. Political control was not always secure or lasting, but cultural influences were strong and pervasive, and if an ethnically different group or tribe adopted the Chinese language, institutions, and Confucian systems of belief, then they were likely to be accepted into the Chinese cultural unity.

The Qin dynasty was the first of China's imperial dynasties and, though it did not last for long, it had enormous influence on the dynasties which followed and the political forms they adopted. Even so, China's history since then has not been one of a simple succession of different imperial houses modelled on the Qin. Interspersed between the longer-lasting dynasties were periods, sometimes of centuries, when the empire was split apart and ravaged by war.

The dynasties which most Westerners have heard of are largely the ones where China was (relatively) united – the Han (from whence comes the term 'Han Chinese'), the Tang (famous for its poetry, in particular), the Song (notable because of developments in Neo-Confucian philosophy), the Yuan (the Mongol dynasty descended from Genghis Khan), the Ming (well-known particularly for its blue and white porcelain) and the Qing.

It was the Qing dynasty, whose ruling élite came from the Manchu tribes of the north-east, which suffered the brunt of Western influence in China, tottered under the impact of such events as the two Opium Wars with Britain during the nineteenth century, and eventually collapsed in the early years of this century. The Republic which followed it in 1912 was itself destroyed by a combination of warlordism, civil war and the war to resist Japanese invasion, and in 1949 it was replaced by the Communist regime of the People's Republic of China (PRC).

THE CHINESE DYNASTIES

(Xia	Legendary)
Shang	c.1700 BC – ?1027 BC
Zhou	?1027 BC – 256 BC
Qin	221 – 209 BC
Han	206 BC – 220 AD
Three Kingdoms	220 – 280
Jin	265 – 420
Southern & Northern Dynasties	420 – 589
Sui	589 – 618
Tang	618 – 907
Five Dynasties	907 – 960
Song	960 – 1279
Yuan (Mongols)	1279 – 1368
Ming	1368 – 1644
Qing (Manchus)	1644 – 1912
Republic of China	1912 – 1949
PRC	1949 –

(The precision of these dates obscures the fact that in many cases there was considerable overlap as a dynasty gradually extended its control over areas ruled by the previous dynasty).

2

The People

'94% are of the Han race'

The PRC was founded in 1949, as a Communist state under Mao Zedong. It now has a population of 1.2 billion, of which some 94% are of the Han race (i.e. what Westerners usually think of as 'Chinese'). The remaining 6% are made up of more than 50 minority nationalities, including Tibetans, Uyghurs, Koreans, Dai, Miao and Yao.

Also in 1949, Chiang Kai-shek and his defeated Nationalist army retreated from mainland China to the island of Taiwan (formerly known as Formosa), and set up their own Republican government there. The population of Taiwan now stands at 21 million, of whom the vast majority are Han Chinese (including both the pre-1949 inhabitants of the island and the mainlanders who moved there in 1949, plus their descendants). There are also non-Han aboriginal groups such as the Ami, who live in the centre and south of Taiwan.

It is important to remember that, in theory at least, both mainland Chinese and the inhabitants of Taiwan see China as one single nation: the PRC see Taiwan as being under enemy occupation, and vice versa.

THE 'OVERSEAS CHINESE'

Pressure of population in China itself, plus invasions, civil wars and economic problems, has meant that for several centuries there has been a steady flow of Chinese people leaving China and settling elsewhere. Initially, Chinese emigrants tended to be traders and craftsmen, who moved to Southeast Asia and were often assimilated into the local population. Later, in the nineteenth century, labourers or 'coolies' (from the Chinese words *ku li*, or 'bitter strength') were recruited in very large numbers from south China for work in British, French and Dutch colonies, and in the Americas.

By the 1930s, there were nearly ten million overseas Chinese, and although such large-scale immigration was halted, many of the descendants of those labourers still live in Chinese communities in their adopted countries today.

Rates of assimilation have varied, and in some of these countries, particularly in Southeast Asia, there has been alarm at the growth of the Chinese population and concern as to where their loyalties lie. (Some communities of ethnic Chinese may have become fully assimilated citizens of their new country, for example, but others may still hold Chinese passports, whether PRC or Taiwanese.) There have been many instances of anti-Chinese legislation, as well as more violent forms of protest. In Malaysia, for example, where some 35% of the total population is Chinese, there are inevitably certain tensions between the communities.

The story is rather different in Singapore, where three-quarters of the population are ethnically Chinese. The island state is hugely successful economically, but even so has to tread warily in its relations both with the PRC and with its Southeast Asian neighbours, in case such success rings alarm bells there.

Hong Kong and Macau are different again, of course, since (until 1997) they are European colonies within China. Hong Kong in particular, with its population of some six million Chinese, is of enormous value to the economy of China and a key link between China and the countries of Southeast Asia. It still preserves many facets of traditional Chinese life and society and is a fascinating window into pre-modern customs as well as a show-case for the latest technologies.

Elsewhere, in the larger cities of the Americas, Western Europe, Japan and Australia, Chinese communities make up only a small percentage of the population, albeit often a very successful one. Historical links tend to have shaped the various Chinese communities – for example, the fact that Hong Kong has been a British colony for over a century means that the majority of the ethnic Chinese in Britain come from there (though originally from southern China); many of the Chinese from Vietnam have emigrated to France; and there is a tendency for Taiwanese Chinese to move to the USA when they emigrate, because of the long-standing support which the US has given the Republic of China.

3

The Foreigner in China

The character 'Monkey' from Chinese opera

As a foreigner in China, it is unlikely that you will ever be taken for a Chinese, and therefore allowances will be made for you. But it is still a good idea to watch what Chinese people do in certain social and business situations and to try and behave in a way not incompatible with this. Expectations are likely to be a good deal higher, however, if the visitor is ethnically of Chinese origin, and this can sometimes lead to problems, and genuine incredulity when it emerges that he/she cannot speak Mandarin.

The Chinese are very keen not to be seen to 'lose face' and this explains many of their behaviour patterns. Laughter, for instance, does not necessarily mean that the person laughing finds something funny (although it may, of course, mean just that): it is often used to cover up embarrassment in an awkward situation, and could mean that the visitor has said something that has not been understood, or the Chinese person is unsure of his ground on some point.

Equally, a foreigner loses face by becoming angry or upset. Impatience is seen by the Chinese as a serious character flaw. In the PRC, in particular, there is an immense amount of red tape involved in what to us might seem the simplest of procedures – buying plane tickets, or changing money at a bank, for example – and it is essential to learn to accept such inconveniences gracefully. Trying to stick to a tight schedule in China is often just not possible.

On meeting someone in China, the usual practice is to shake hands, often for a much longer time than would be the norm in the West. This may be accompanied by a respectful nod. If you are being introduced to a group of people, make sure to shake hands with all of them. From then on, as far as physical contact is concerned, take your cue from the person you are talking to.

If you are dealing with someone of the opposite sex, there is unlikely to be any touching after the initial handshake, but members of the same sex do tend to touch each other more than in the West, and women frequently emphasize a point by patting each other on the arm. In some places away from large urban centres, you may well see young people of the same sex walking along the street hand in hand: in Chinese society this is no more than an expression of friendship. (There are homosexuals in China, as everywhere else, but this is not publicly acknowledged. The whole topic is considered rather shocking.)

Chinese people rise early and retire early, so lunch will probably be at noon and evening banquets are likely to begin at six. Once the meal is over (and it could last for a fairly long time), the visitors may chat for a few minutes but should then get up and go. There is none of the prolonged after-dinner coffee-drinking so common in the West, and departure soon after the end of the meal is the rule in China.

4

Hotels, Sightseeing & Money

'Comfortable. . .joint-venture hotels'

Most visitors to China are likely to be staying in hotels. In the bigger cities, in both the PRC and Taiwan, there are numerous very modern hotels where standards of comfort are easily on a par with many top hotels in the West, but outside these cities standards can vary considerably.

In the PRC, the most comfortable hotels are usually the joint-venture hotels, built with large injections of foreign capital and managed, generally speaking, either by Westerners or Hong Kong Chinese. Also first-class are the top Chinese hotels, but service here can be a bit patchy. Both these sorts of hotels provide private bathrooms, mini-bars, TV, laundry service, IDD telephone service, and sometimes swimming-pools etc. There are usually several restaurants to choose from, offering European as well as Chinese cuisine, and often a range of shops from bakers to hairdressers.

You will have to register when you arrive, so keep your passport handy. And it is a good idea to label all your luggage clearly, as mix-ups have been known to occur. If you have any valuables with you, you can check them into the hotel safe.

The third category of hotel which visitors to the PRC are likely to use are the tourist hotels. These are much less glamorous, and cheaper. They are often older too, and although quite clean may have rather idiosyncratic plumbing. As in the other two categories of hotel, Western breakfast should be available, but here it usually reflects the fact that the cooks are Chinese. There will be a service desk on each floor, but the service personnel will not necessarily speak English. There will probably by a TV in each room, and there will also be flasks of boiling water and Chinese tea in packets. Be prepared for the fact that some of these hotels do not accept credit cards.

Although most Westerners visiting China will use Western-style hotels, where the lavatories in the bathrooms will be similar to the ones they have at home, it is quite likely that they will come across Chinese-style lavatories when out and about on sightseeing trips, factory visits etc., and so details of them are included here. A Chinese lavatory consists of a porcelain trough set in the floor, over which one has to squat, feet on either side, facing the end where there is a kind of hood. In the PRC there is usually no lavatory paper (remember to take some with you) and even if there is, the Chinese usually require you to throw it into a special bin after use rather than to flush it down the pan. (This seems to be partly because of the limitations of the sewage system, but also because the Chinese in the PRC use what is euphemistically referred to as 'night-soil' as fertilizer, and they do not want strands of paper spread all over their fields with it.) As a result, public lavatories in China and sometimes even the communal ones in hotels, have a very distinctive and unpleasant smell and are not places in which to linger.

SIGHTSEEING

Numerous books have been published on this topic, of course. As is widely known, much of the sightseeing is organized by tour operators, or from your hotel, and in the PRC can include factories as well as the usual temples (most of them refurbished rather hastily in the last few years), palaces, museums and so on.

On the whole, such visits are straightforward and demand no special behaviour. But remember that it is polite to ask permission before you take a photograph of a person (even though this may result in a request for a small payment). Photographers are not always welcome. In temples, be especially sensitive – there may be people worshipping – and try not to cause too much of a stir by your presence. Dress appropriately and keep your voice down.

Travelling by taxi to your destination is probably the way most business visitors or tourists will choose, but it can still present unforeseen problems. Most taxi-drivers, whether in the PRC or in Taiwan, speak no English, so it is advisable to ask someone in your hotel to write down your destination in Chinese so that you can show it to the driver. In the PRC you may occasionally find that a taxi-driver refuses to take you in his cab, but it makes no sense to argue. One just has be to philosophical about it, as about many things in China which are different from home.

Once you get into the cab, make sure that the driver starts the meter running, and remember to do up your seat-belt. Driving can be erratic and, especially in Taiwan, traffic accidents are very common.

Tipping is officially prohibited in the PRC, and used never to occur, but in recent years, especially in the south, some service personnel have begun to make it plain that tips are expected. In Taiwan, they are usually added to one's bill: if not, the norm is probably 10–15%.

MONEY

Gone, thank heavens, are the days when foreigners in the PRC had to pay for everything in FEC (Foreign Exchange Certificates, popularly known among Westerners as 'funny money'). Nowadays, all cash transactions are in Renminbi ('people's currency'), and this is what you will be given when you change your money at the airport or at banks or hotels. (It is not possible to buy Renminbi outside China.) US dollars are much in demand, but remember that the illegal money-changers who accost you in the street, and who seem to be active all over China, could get you into serious trouble.

Exchange rates seem to be much the same wherever you change money, so do not waste time shopping around. There are branches of many Western banks in Beijing now, but you should not have difficulty in changing travellers' cheques etc. in branches of The Bank of China, or in your hotel.

A word of advice. Credit cards, although increasingly widespread in use, are not yet as commonly acceptable in China as in the West, so you may want to carry more cash on you than you normally would. (Watch out for pickpockets, however – also an increasingly widespread phenomenon.)

In Taiwan, the currency is the New Taiwan dollar. These are only available within Taiwan and you can exchange cash/travellers' cheques for them at the airport when you arrive.

In both the PRC and Taiwan, you should keep the receipts for your money-changing transactions so that you have no problems changing the local currency back into pounds/dollars when you leave the country.

Chinese-style lavatory

5

Communication and Making Friends

'Chinese people are often more direct'

NAMES

Remember that in China the surname *precedes* the personal name, since the family group or clan has traditionally been seen as more important than the individual. Zhang Hua is thus Mr Zhang, not Mr Hua. In addressing the Chinese people you meet it is best to use Mr, Mrs, Miss plus their surnames: Chinese people are more formal than many Westerners. ('Comrade' seems to have dropped out of use in recent years. It was only ever used in the PRC, but if you use it there now you may find that it makes people laugh.)

You may also find that the Chinese refer to one another by their job-title – Mayor Wang, Manager Li and so on. This is a direct translation of the way they would normally refer to one another in Chinese, and you might find it a useful habit to adopt, because you are almost bound to meet several people who share the same surname, and it will help you keep them separate in your mind.

Most Chinese surnames, of which there are only a few hundred, are of one syllable only, and some of the commonest are Zhang, Wang, Wu, Zhao and Li. Personal names can be of either one or two syllables and are very often chosen according to a pre-arranged plan, sometimes one which the family has adhered to for generations. The children of each generation – and this includes those cousins who are children of one's father's brothers – may all have a 'generation' characters in common: Li Weiguang, for instance, may have a younger brother or cousin called Li Weiguo and a sister called Li Weiling, where Li is the family's surname and Wei the 'generation' character.

These days, however, complications can arise when Chinese people start choosing Western names for themselves. They are, of course, quite right in thinking that 'James Chen' is easier for a Western visitor to remember than, say, Chen Jianrong. Particularly in Hong Kong, you are likely to come across many a 'Peter Wong' or 'Ivy Mao', or even the odd 'Ribena Lo' or 'Rolex Chan'*, but this habit of reversing the order of surname/personal name

---

* The *pinyin* system of romanization is not used in Hong Kong, where the vast majority of the population speak Cantonese, not Mandarin.

is occasionally carried over into their Chinese names too. So it is a good idea, especially when confronted with a Chinese name of only two syllables, such as Jing Wang, to check whether the bearer of that name is a Mr/Ms *Jing*, or a Mr/Ms *Wang*.

CONVERSATION

B ecause of upheavals in the education system during the Cultural Revolution and afterwards, the amount of English which your Chinese contacts know will vary considerably. Some of them may know no English at all, having learnt Russian or Japanese at school, but even those who do know some English will almost invariably have had much less practice in speaking the language than in reading or writing it.

S o, be patient, use short sentences, speak a little more slowly than usual if you suspect you are not being understood, and try not to use unnecessarily difficult words, or slang. Be prepared to re-phrase what you have just said, rather than just repeat it, and be sure not to raise your voice. In Taiwan especially, many Chinese people are more attuned to an American pronunciation than to an English one.

I f you are using an interpreter, try not to say too much at a time – give her (or him) a chance to interpret a manageable amount before you move onto the next sentence. It is important to maintain eye-contact with the person you are dealing with (though not all the time, of course), rather than solely with the interpreter.

A lthough in accounts of traditional China Western writers often used to make the point that Chinese people were not given to being direct in conversation and favoured the oblique approach to almost all subjects, in fact you will probably find that the Chinese people you meet, while still treating you very courteously, are often more direct than many Westerners. You can expect to be asked questions about your age, marital status and salary – and you, in turn, can ask them about the same sorts of things.

If you are in the PRC, remember to be a little cautious (and sensitive) when talking about the number of children someone has. The government's one-child policy has caused an enormous amount of anguish, and is best touched on lightly unless the person you are talking to appears to want to pursue the subject.

I, personally, am also quite careful when asked what my salary is, and tend to answer jokingly along the lines of 'Not enough'. This is simply to avoid the embarrassment of disclosing a sum which to the vast majority of China's population still seems incredibly high.

There is a tremendous curiosity about the West in the PRC. This is probably because of the long period of isolation from it that China underwent after the Communist take-over in 1949. It also means that the Chinese tend to seize every opportunity they can to practise their English. Do not be surprised if you are accosted in the street by young people who produce one or two sentences in English and then, overcome by embarrassment, lapse into silence. You may be the first foreigner they have ever seen, let alone spoken to. In many cities there is an 'English corner' held in the park on Sundays, and you may be invited along to help.

In many of the less frequently visited areas of China, you may find that the local people, especially the children, are absolutely fascinated by such Western characteristics as blonde hair, blue eyes, or hairy arms. It can make you feel very self-conscious when they come up and touch you or feel your hair, but there is not a lot you can do about it except smile politely.

You may often see Chinese people blowing their noses between their fingers onto the pavement. This is not considered bad manners. Spitting is also very common, although there have been campaigns against it for reasons of hygiene. Belching, especially just after a meal, is something else not considered rude, and in fact, is usually supposed to indicate a feeling of well-being.

SOME TABOOS

Japan

A word of warning about the attitude of many of the Chinese people to the Japanese might be in order here. Although it would be denied in public, especially in view of the enormous investments which Japan is now making in China, in private many Chinese people do not hesitate to admit that the Japanese are intensely disliked. This dates back to the Sino-Japanese War of 1894-5, but particularly also to Japan's invasion of China in the 1930s, including the occupation of Manchuria and the rape of Nanjing (Nanking) in 1937. For this reason, it might be wise to avoid being too lavish in your praise of Japan.

This caveat also applies when talking to former mainlanders who are now in

Taiwan, of course, but you may find that the native Taiwanese Chinese and the aboriginal peoples there do not share such feelings towards the Japanese, as although they were under Japanese occupation for fifty years, until 1945, this did actually bring some practical benefits in terms of education etc.

Hong Kong

The subject of Hong Kong has, of course, become rather a touchy one in the past few years and at least for the time being, I would suggest that, unless your Chinese contacts are quite well-known to you, or they themselves bring it up, it would be easier for all concerned to try and avoid it.

Tibet

Another thorny topic. Most Chinese people know little or nothing about the abuses of human rights which continue to be perpetrated by the Chinese regime in Tibet, and this is not a subject which will ease relations with your Chinese contacts.

'Gateway to the Forbidden City'

Home Life, Visits & Presents

'. . .an even bigger present would be in order'

If you are fortunate enough to have made friends with a Chinese person on an individual basis, you will soon realize that there is no such concept in China as 'going Dutch'. You can offer to pay for both of you – on the bus, say, or going to the cinema – but not just for yourself. Your offer will almost certainly be refused, in which case the thing to do is offer to pay on the journey back, next time, etc. You may find that your offers are always refused, however, because the Chinese believe that they should not allow a 'foreign guest' to pay for anything while in China.

A gain, if you have Chinese friends you may be lucky enough to be invited to a Chinese home, although in the PRC it is very rare for this to happen. (I am not referring here to the kind of artificial 'visit to the masses' which has often been included in tours of China.) There could be several reasons for this: shortage of space is the one most often quoted, but other considerations may be distance, insecurity about having dealings with foreigners in the first place, and feelings of inferiority with regard to material possessions. It goes without saying, therefore, that one has to show great tact and consideration here, especially concerning the last two points.

D epending on which way the political wind is blowing, many Chinese in the PRC can be quite wary of being seen to consort with foreigners. If you visit someone in their own flat, you will very probably have to pass beneath the watchful eye of the concierge at the door, and may have to sign in when you arrive and out when you leave, so that there is a record of your visit. This is one reason your Chinese friends might prefer to entertain you elsewhere.

A s to the difference in personal possessions, although in many families this gap is now narrowing (especially in Taiwan, where the growth of a wealthy middle-class has meant that more homes are now equipped with all modern conveniences and are as comfortable as middle-class homes in the West), many homes are still rather basic by Western standards. You will see plenty of colour TVs, refrigerators etc., but much of the furniture in Chinese houses can look old-fashioned or ill-designed to a Westerner, the lighting is usually fluorescent, and even new buildings look very poorly finished.

Even though Taiwan has been prospering rapidly for quite a long time now, it is still not very common for a foreigner to be invited to a private home, unless he or she has been in Taiwan for a while and knows the Chinese hosts well. If you are invited, be prepared to take off your shoes just after you enter the door and put on the slippers provided for you – many families have preserved this custom from the time when the island was occupied by the Japanese.

Some families still live in Japanese-style houses (though these are rapidly being replaced by modern developments), and many of them have at least one room where the floor is covered with *tatami* (the thick, standard-size rush mats found so commonly in Japan.) These have to be treated carefully, as they cannot really be cleaned: hence the need to remove your shoes. (Try to remember not to wear socks with holes in them!) In the PRC floors are usually made of concrete, with maybe a rug or mat on top. Slippers may be provided here too.

PRESENTS

When Chinese visitors come to the West they invariably bring a number of small, typically Chinese presents for their hosts, and this custom is a good one to imitate. For the most senior of the people you will be dealing with, a bigger present would be in order, though if it is at all sizeable it might be a good idea to make it plain that you giving it to him for the whole of his group or organiza-tion. Otherwise, suitable gifts could be com-pany pens (with refills, if needed), or company ties, ashtrays, small pieces of glass (e.g. paperweights) or Wedgwood. Whisky (the better brands) and foreign cigarettes go down well, but Chinese people tend not to be as fond of sweets as we are, so chocolates are out, and so are flowers. Your interpreter would probably appreciate a book or two.

Whatever you do, avoid giving clocks or watches as presents. This is important, as the words for 'to give a clock' sound exactly the same as the words for 'to take someone to their death'.

Street market

7

Doing Business

'First. . .exchange business cards'

As noted earlier, whole books have been written on doing business with China, and so no mention will be made here of how to conduct negotiations. But it is worth bringing up one or two points which fall more appropriately under the rubric of etiquette.

These days, there is a new confidence and pride in China and Westerners should be very careful not to behave as if they were superior to the Chinese. Those Chinese who deal with foreigners are very aware of China's attraction for potential business partners, but they are also very knowledgeable about technology, international pricing and world markets etc. It would be a mistake to treat them as some sort of 'poor relation'.

When you go to a business meeting, the first thing that happens is an exchange of business cards. When someone hands you his card, make sure to read it, not just glance at it and put it away. You may well find it helpful to place the cards you receive on the table in front of you, so that it is easier to remind yourself of the names of your Chinese counterparts.

It is a good idea to take along a large stock of your own cards, if possible with a Chinese version of your name and position within your company on the back. If you cannot get the cards made locally (for instance, through an airline or translation agency), you can probably have them printed in your own local 'Chinatown', or else in Hong Kong if you pass through, or you can ask the reception desk in your hotel for help in finding a reliable printer after you get to China.

Do try to get whoever chooses your name for you to keep it to two or three syllables – anything longer could be difficult for the Chinese to manage. And remember that the simplified forms of the Chinese characters which are now in use in the PRC are not used in Taiwan or Hong Kong. Check this when you order your cards from the printer.

Dress should be quite formal – for men, suits and ties are best, though some Western business men do wear safari-suits, especially in hot weather. It is quite acceptable for women to wear trousers, as many Chinese women do, but skirts or suits are widely perceived as smarter. Make-up, too, is now used quite frequently by younger Chinese women.

The Chinese are very status-conscious, so it is best to remember, when dealing with a group, that they will come into the room in order of seniority. (It may be that the actual negotiations are carried out by someone other than the most senior member, however.) Make sure to shake hands with all of them – it is impolite to shake hands with only the first few and then give up. You will no doubt notice that there is no custom of giving precedence to the female members of the group.

When engaged in business dealings, as in other situations, a Chinese person may feel that a direct 'no' would be embarrassing to both parties, and try to convey his disagreement by more indirect methods, such as evading the question or remaining silent. The Western businessman will need to be sensitive to this, and learn to interpret the signals which his Chinese counterpart is giving out. In some cases, of course, what appears to be an attempt at stalling may genuinely mean that the person you are dealing with has to consult his superiors, but in other cases it may be a sign that concessions on your part are required if the discussions are to go much further. Be prepared for the Chinese side to request changes to a contract after it has been signed.

Although most business entertaining is done in restaurants, it is not usual for spouses to be invited along. If your spouse is in China with you, she/he can expect to have to amuse herself/himself on the evenings when there are banquets and so on, unless specifically included in the invitation.

Punctuality is considered very important when doing business in China. The people with whom you are dealing will not keep you waiting, and you should make a point of being on time too. Equally, it is important that you should not keep looking at your watch and implying that you are in a great hurry to finish a deal.

After your arrival in China, any arrangements for your travel within the country will usually be taken care of by the organization you are visiting. You will probably be met by representatives of this organization when you arrive, whether at the airport or the railway station, and you will also probably be seen off by them when you leave. More senior members of the organization are likely to say goodbye to you at your hotel, while relatively junior members will escort you all the way to your point of departure. This is the custom in China, and not a mark of any special esteem.

Once you have returned from China to your own country, it would be a nice gesture to remember your Chinese contacts the following Christmas (or, preferably, New Year) by sending them small gifts, such as calendars, or cards. This will be much appreciated.

WOMEN VISITING CHINA

Foreign women visiting China will have no occasion to feel ill at ease simply because they are female. There may not be equal numbers of men and women in all occupations or at all levels in China, but there are, in theory at any rate, equal opportunities for both sexes, and the Chinese are quite happy to deal with both men and women, in business or as tourists.

Women who frequently visit the PRC on business report that they are well accepted by their male Chinese counterparts and that it is not considered odd if they reciprocate toasts at banquets and so on. They should dress modestly, (no sun-dresses or low necklines, for example) and should not behave in too extrovert a manner. 'Loud' behaviour or flashiness in either sex does not go down well in China. Especially in the less cosmopolitan areas of the PRC, foreigners will be stared at constantly, and it is obviously not a good idea to draw even more attention to oneself by inappropriate behaviour.

Women in China very rarely drink alcohol, so that if a Western woman prefers to drink non-alcoholic drinks no-one will be at all surprised or put out. Female visitors should also bear in mind that although there are now some Western-style chemist shops in the big cities of the PRC, these can be extremely expensive, and so they may wish to equip themselves with all the cosmetics, toilet articles etc. that they require before they set out from home. (This is not such a problem in Taiwan, though prices can still be rather high.)

'. . .no occasion to feel ill at ease'

8

Leisure Activities

Lion Dance

As the economic boom continues in the Chinese world, there is an ever-increasing variety of entertainment and leisure activities available. Apart from cinemas, theatres, and food outlets (pizza and burgers are all the rage), there are *karaoke* clubs, MTV lounges, and night-clubs. There are often a number of 'hostesses' in these places, both Chinese and Western (especially in the PRC, young women from the former Soviet Union). They tend to be heavily made-up and provocatively dressed – the Communist puritanism of the past is long gone – and can be very willing to help their customers spend large amounts of cash. There is a lot of money about in Chinese cities these days, and it shows.

SHOPPING

Shopping is another leisure activity in which the Chinese themselves are now able to indulge. A few years ago, tourists in the PRC were invariably pointed in the direction of the 'Friendship Store' when they wanted to buy anything. These stores stocked a wider range of goods (usually 'typical' Chinese products like silk blouses, paintings, fans, cloisonné, jewellery etc.) and better-quality merchandise than most of the ordinary department stores where the Chinese people would do their shopping. However, with the advent of joint-venture shopping centres and a much freer market for consumer goods, the breath of competition has swept through China and there is a much wider variety of goods available at a far larger number of outlets than used to be the case.

It is not acceptable to haggle over prices in the shops (though it has been known), but in the free markets it is perfectly all right – if one can overcome the language barrier, of course! And these days, many of the street traders can speak enough English to make a successful sale.

EATING OUT

Although meals are included in the overall arrangements for most people who visit China (and here I am referring to both Taiwan and the PRC) on business or as tourists, and will be taken either in the hotels they stay in or at restaurants known to their business contacts or the tour operator, it is nevertheless interesting to venture out and eat elsewhere. Independent travellers find that this is one of the best ways to experience the 'real' China. You need to be willing to communicate on your own by gestures and good humour, since you cannot necessarily expect to find anyone who speaks English (and, depending where you are, the very arrival of a foreigner may well cause consternation in the first place), but you would be surprised how easy it is once you try.

In the PRC, and sometimes in Taiwan too, be prepared for levels of hygiene in restaurants to be far below those of the West – the floor may be littered with chicken-bones, for example – and for rather unpredictable standards of service. The state-run restaurants are well-known for their scowling and unhelpful staff, but these days there are more and more small, family-run restaurants opening up in the cities of the PRC, and food here is often good, as well as cheap, while service is usually friendly. In Taiwan, food is much more expensive than it used to be, but it is still generally of a high standard and there is probably more choice of cuisine within a given city.

Vegetarians can sometimes run into problems in China, where the concept of not eating meat is a very novel one. Try to explain that you eat only vegetables and bean-curd (*doufu*), but watch out for meat stock and bits of fat in all sorts of dishes.

A VISIT TO THE OPERA

A uniquely Chinese form of entertainment is, of course, the Beijing (Peking) opera. It is a form of traditional Chinese drama that has been popular for about 150 years, and involves acrobatics, fencing and boxing as well as music and singing. The music may sound very harsh and discordant to the

Western ear, but the whole thing is definitely a spectacle worth seeing, even if only once.

The characters on stage wear splendid costumes and colourful, stylized make-up, but the audience, too, is worth watching. They will virtually all know the story, and probably the music too, of the opera, and this means they feel free to get up and walk about during the performance, chat to their friends, buy and eat snacks and generally behave in a way quite different from the average opera audience in the West.

FESTIVALS

There were many festivals in the traditional Chinese lunar calendar, and several of these are still celebrated throughout the Chinese world. The most important, and the most widely known in the West, is **Chinese New Year**. (In the PRC this is known as **Spring Festival**, because New Year is officially 1 January.) This has always been the time for family reunions. It falls during the slack period of the farming year (remember that in the PRC more than three-quarters of the population are still engaged in agriculture) and this means that almost everyone can snatch a few days holiday.

The atmosphere is very festive – everyone dresses in new clothes, strings of fire-crackers are let off (the tradition is that this will scare away any evil spirits lurking around, and also welcome in the new year – but recently the use of fire-crackers has been restricted in the cities of the PRC) and there is a lot of feasting.

Families will make, and eat, hundreds of *jiaozi* (stuffed dumplings which are supposed to be shaped like gold ingots and therefore to bring good luck) and they will eat much more meat than usual, and perhaps a special sticky New Year cake called *niangao*. Younger members of the family should pay their respects to the older members (and, in more traditional homes, to the ancestors as well), and the children will be given small red envelopes of money.

A lot of visiting goes on between relatives and friends, and houses are decorated with special New Year pictures and matching couplets written on red paper. In many places, this will also be the occasion to watch a **Lion Dance**, and for all-night gambling sessions. It is also a time for payment of debts.

Other festivals you may hear about include the **Dragon Boat Festival** (Duan Yang Jie or Duan Wu Jie) and the mid-Autumn Festival. The former falls on the fifth day of the fifth lunar month. It is a very ancient festival whose origins have been lost in the mists of time, but these days it is associated with Qu Yuan, a loyal minister of Chu (an ancient state in the south of China) who committed suicide in the third century BC by jumping into a local river when the king of Chu refused to listen to his good advice.

There are lively races between long, thin 'dragon boats' to the rhythm of drums, and these are said by some people to represent attempts to rescue Qu Yuan. Special packets of glutinous rice (*zongzi*) wrapped in leaves are eaten, and again, these are said to have been intended for the fish (or, in some versions, the dragon) in the river, so that they would eat them and leave Qu Yuan alone.

The Mid-Autumn Festival occurs on the 15th day of the eighth lunar month, at a time when the moon is supposed to be brighter and fuller than at any other time of the year. This, too, is a festival when the family gets together, possibly to sing folk-songs (or, these days, karaoke), or to display fancy lanterns, but mostly to admire the moon and eat 'mooncakes'. These are round cakes stuffed with a variety of things such as lotus-seed paste, fruit or nuts, ham or egg-yolks. (The fillings vary according to the different areas of China.)

There are also a number of festivals which fall at specified times of the solar calendar. In the PRC, for instance, as well as **Labour Day** on 1 May, there is **Chinese Youth Day** on 4 May, **Army Day** on 1 August and **National Day** on 1 October. (In Taiwan, National Day is 10 October. They also celebrate such days as **Confucius' Birthday** on 28 September, and **Constitution Day**, 25 December.)

TRAVEL WITHIN CHINA

China is a vast country and most visitors will find that the quickest way to cover long distances is by air. The Chinese have a rather dismaying record on air safety for domestic flights, but as they open up more airports and invest in better equipment this can only improve. Flying is, however, relatively expensive and not as interesting as travelling by train.

Rail travel is the way most Chinese people get around the country, but be warned that getting tickets can be extremely difficult and needs to be done well in advance of your trip. Your ticket is good for one train only, so do not miss it! Travel by train is not fast (not even the 'express' trains), but it gives the traveller a much better idea of what China is really like.

The rail network is huge and seems to be permanently overcrowded. You can travel 'soft'-class or 'hard'-class, but either way you will be expected, as a foreigner, to pay much more than a Chinese person would.

Soft-class accommodation is very comfortable, with four berths in the sleeping compartments and air-conditioning. Hard sleepers are arranged in serried ranks in a sort of dormitory car but are also comfortable, if rather lacking in privacy. Least comfortable, and certainly not to be recommended for journeys of more than a few hours, is hard-seat accommodation. This is usually dangerously overcrowded by Western standards and although providing an unparalleled insight into Chinese life is not for the faint-hearted.

It is possible to travel by long-distance bus in China, but again this is not very comfortable, especially if you are likely to have a lot of baggage crammed around your knees. Travel by boat is also quite common and can be very enjoyable – there are regular boats along the Yangzi river (through the famous gorges), along the Grand Canal, and up the Pearl River from Canton (Guangzhou) to Wuzhou.

Curiously shaped peaks along the River Li,
Guilin region of Guangxi

9

Banquets and Being Entertained

'Banquets. . .a regular feature of life'

Banquets are a regular feature of life for the business person visiting China, especially if there is a group of you, and they can consist of up to a dozen courses, so it is a good idea to pace yourself carefully. In the north of China, soup is often served at the end of the meal, which will usually begin with a dish of cold hors d'oeuvres, but in the south of China soup may be served as the first course. (The Chinese do not, as a rule, eat dessert, although fresh fruit may be provided – usually oranges cut into pieces.) If there is any rice, it will not be served until near the end of the meal: it is seen as a 'filler', in case your guests are still hungry, and therefore it is polite to leave some of it in your bowl, to show that you have been well-fed and have no need of anything more.

The Chinese host, who usually sits facing the door, will place the most eminent guest in the seat of honour, i.e. to his right, and the deputy Chinese host will place the next most senior guest on *his* right, at the opposite side of the table. If there is an interpreter, he/she will probably be seated to the right of the most important guest. Hosts and guests will normally be seated alternately round the table.

When you sit down at the table, you are unlikely to find a knife and fork laid for you, so be prepared to try eating with chopsticks. (It is useful to have practised this prior to departure for China, but even if you have done this, asking for a demonstration from your hosts can be a helpful way of breaking the ice.) And watch what the Chinese diners do when they help themselves to the communal dish of food – they may use a serving spoon, but it is very common to use one's own chopsticks. Do not be surprised if your host is continually placing the tastiest morsels on your plate – this is one way of honouring a guest, who should always wait to be urged to eat before helping himself.

Before and/or after the meal you may be given a hot damp towel to wipe your hands with. (Men can also mop their faces, but this is not usually done by women.) If it is given to you before the meal, you can use it as a napkin for sticky fingers through the rest of the meal. If you find a bone or a piece of gristle in your mouth and want to remove it, use your chopsticks or the porcelain soup spoon, *not* your fingers. The Chinese themselves would spit it out, so that, too, would be acceptable.

As to lifting your bowl (of soup, rice, etc.) towards your mouth, that also is perfectly all right. The key to a relaxed evening is really just to watch what your hosts do when they eat and copy them. But since you are the guest, do not put food onto *their* plates.

Speeches, and their concluding toasts, usually happen quite soon after the beginning of the meal. The host will probably speak between the first and second courses, and the chief guest should reply a few minutes later, after the start of the second course. Take a lead from your host, keep your speech short – perhaps just a few general appreciative comments and some remarks about future cooperation, friendly ties between your organizations and so on – and above all, avoid elaborate jokes (often untranslatable, or at least no longer funny once they have been translated).

One other thing to remember during a banquet: do not take the easy option and spend the entire time conversing with your Western colleagues. This would be very impolite. Talking to your Chinese hosts may seem difficult to begin with, but can be very rewarding. Food is one good topic of conversation, and the discussion of the relative merits of different places in China is another.

If you are in China for more than a couple of days, it is a good idea to arrange a return banquet for your Chinese hosts before you leave. Ask your interpreter, or whoever is organizing your visit, about this, and remember to keep time free for it. A table-plan should be drawn up, and at the banquet there should be place-cards. A supply of foreign cigarettes is always welcome on such occasions. And do remember to keep plying your guests with food. They will be very loath to help themselves and will often decline something offered to them several times before they feel able to accept, so you will have to keep pressing them to eat. These days you may find that you are expected to pay for several meals rather than just one.

ALCOHOL AND TEA

Alcohol is very important at banquets and formal meals. (The Chinese tend not to drink without food.) You will probably find three glasses beside your plate, one for the very good lager-type beer which is commonly drunk and is not very strong, one for some kind of wine (either of the vermouth-type, or, in the PRC, one of the rather sweet and syrupy grape wines produced there) and a small one for a more fiery liquor, such as *maotai*, which is distilled from sorghum and is 65–70° proof. The *maotai* is usually used for toasts and you will often see the Chinese finish off a whole glass each time.

The Chinese equivalent of 'Cheers' is *ganbei* (literally, dry glasses), but caution is advisable here because there are often a number of toasts. It should also be pointed out that the consumption of large amounts of alcohol at such meals is being officially discouraged. If you do not want to drink alcohol, orange squash (fizzy) and mineral water are usually available. (No one drinks tap-water unless it has been boiled.)

The Chinese drink large quantities of tea (mostly 'green tea', as opposed to the 'black' tea which is more commonly drunk in the West) and they add no milk or sugar. In general, it is consumed at meetings and at work rather than in restaurants and at formal meals. It is usually served in mugs with lids. Cigarette smoking is widespread, though much less so among women, and cigarettes are almost always offered along with the tea. To a Westerner, it is rather surprising that most Chinese people do not seem to be at all worried about the links between smoking and health problems.

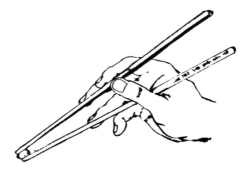

Using chopsticks

10

Medical Matters

Acupuncture and 'vital energy'

VISITING A DOCTOR

If you fall ill in China, you should be able to arrange a visit to the doctor through the staff at your hotel. In the PRC this might entail a trip to the local hospital, but this is only because there is no such person as a GP in China. It is very worrying for the Chinese, who see themselves as your hosts for as long as you are in their country, to have a sick foreigner on their hands, and they will make every effort to see that you are well cared for.

Standards of care do vary, however, and you would be well-advised to take with you a supply of any medicines and pharmaceutical products you think you may need. In the PRC, for instance, hypodermic needles are often used more than once, so take some with you in case you need to have an injection of some sort. (Chinese doctors will commonly want to give you an injection for even the most minor ailments, but you can always resist and request some other form of treatment.)

Make sure, before you leave home, that you have adequate insurance cover, as medical care is not free in either Taiwan or the PRC. If you are offered a choice of Western medicine or Chinese medicine, do not automatically feel you must choose the former. Acupuncture in particular (with sterile needles, of course) can be extremely effective for some conditions, as can some of the traditional herbal remedies.

CHINESE MEDICINE

There are several systems of healing which have enjoyed popularity in the Chinese world, of which acupuncture and herbal medicine are probably the two best-known in the West.

Acupuncture involves the insertion of thin needles into points of the body where needling is thought to produce the effects desired. It is especially helpful in relieving pain. According to the theory, one's health depends on having an uninterrupted flow of *qi* (which can be translated as 'vital energy') through the whole organism. If there is too little *qi*, or too much, or if its flow is obstructed in some way, symptoms will appear which require treatment.

Instead of needles, some acupuncturists sometimes use seeds fixed with sticking-plaster to particular points in the ear – you press them hard for a few seconds, three times a day, and the effect is said to be as beneficial as using needles. Some practitioners also perform moxibustion as well as, or instead of, acupuncture. This is the burning of moxa (mugwort) on the surface of the body, for therapeutic reasons.

Herbal medicine is also popular throughout the Chinese world, and even in the West you may have seen a Chinese medicine shop with its tiers of small drawers filled with the various ingredients (animal, vegetable and mineral) which are called for in traditionally-prescribed medicines.

Diagnostic techniques of the traditional Chinese doctor include taking the patient's pulse for several minutes, because the speed and strength of the pulse are believed to indicate certain characteristic states of health. The medicine prescribed will usually involve a number of different substances which have to be simmered together for a long time and will invariably taste horrible. (The Chinese have a saying about bitter medicine being good for you.)

11

Something about the Language: Mandarin

China is such a vast country, and because of her geography transport and communications have always been difficult, so it is not surprising that, over the course of her very long history, several different forms of the Chinese language have developed. These are usually referred to as 'dialects', but since they are in many cases mutually unintelligible, it is more helpful to think of them as separate languages. They include Mandarin, Cantonese, Shanghainese, Hakka, Hokkien (Fukien) and many others.

Mandarin is the language used in both the PRC and Taiwan as the medium of education and the lingua franca. In the PRC it is called *putonghua* (common or standard speech) and in Taiwan it is known as *guoyu* (national language). In theory, anyone under about fifty-five should be able to speak Mandarin – even if they prefer to speak their own local variety of Chinese at home - but in practice this is not always the case. (Written Chinese is largely uniform throughout the country, although in the PRC many of the characters are now written in a simplified form.)

Chinese is a tone-language. This means that differences in the pitch at which a particular syllable is pronounced convey differences in meaning. For example, *tāng* (said on a high level tone) means 'soup', but *táng* said on a rising tone) means 'sugar'; *gŏu* (where the pitch falls and then rises) means 'dog', but *gòu* (said with a falling tone) means 'enough'.

There are four tones in Mandarin:

‾	level (and relatively high)
´	rising
ˇ	fall-rise
`	falling

(Any syllable in the vocabulary list over the page which has *no* tone-mark is spoken so lightly as to be virtually tone-less.)

This may sound complicated, but compared to other dialects which have many more tones, it is remarkably straightforward! For most non-Chinese-speaking people the tones are the greatest obstacle to speaking Chinese correctly. They need a good deal of practice – but, as with using chopsticks, if you ask your

Chinese contacts to help you improve your pronunciation, this can be a useful conversational gambit.

SIMPLE VOCABULARY

nǐ hǎo?	Hello (lit., you well?)
zài jiàn	Goodbye (lit., again see)
xiè xie	Thank you
zǎo	Good morning
huānyíng	Welcome
duìbuqǐ	Sorry, excuse me (not used as much as in English)
Yīnggúo	England
Yīnggúorén	English (person)
Yīnggúohuà, Yīngyǔ	English (language)
Měigúo	America
Měiguórén	American (person)
Zhōnggúo	China
Zhōngguórén	Chinese (person)
Zhōnggúohùa; Hànyǔ (in the PRC)	Chinese (language)
Jiānádà	Canada
Jiānádàrén	Canadian
Aòdàlìyà	Australia
Aòdàlìyàrén	Australian
Xīnxīlán	New Zealand
Xīnxīlánrén	New Zealander
Wǒ bù hùi shūo Zhōnggúohùa	I can't speak Chinese
wǒ shì. . .	I am. . .
. . .zài nǎr?	Where is. . .?
fànguǎnr	Restaurant
lǚgǔan	Hotel
cèsuǒ (in the PRC) *xīshǒujiān* (in Taiwan)	Lavatory

huǒchēzhàn   Railway station
yóujú   Post office

The system of romanization applied in this book is the *pinyin* system which is used in the PRC for textbooks and so on. Foreign learners should remember that they cannot automatically give the letters their usual sounds, however. Many of the sounds in Chinese do approximate English sounds, but there are a number of conventions which have to be observed.

c is pronounced as *ts* in 'cats'
z is pronounced as *ds* in 'seeds'
q is pronounced as *ch* in 'cheap'
j is pronounced as *j* in 'jig'
x is pronounced as something between *sh* in 'shin' and *s*
s as in 'siesta'
r is pronounced as a cross between *s* in 'vision' and *r* in 'red'
h is pronounced as *ch* in Scottish 'loch'
zh is pronounced as *j* in 'July'
a is like *ar* in 'far'
-ang is like *ung* in Southern English 'sung'
e is like *er* in 'her'
en is like *en* in 'stricken'
ei is like *ay* in 'hay'
ou is like *ou* in 'soul'
i is like *ee* in 'see', except after c s z r ch sh and zh, when it is like the *i* in American 'sir'
u is like *oo* in 'soon'
ü is like *e* in 'see' but said with the lips rounded as if for oo
-ong is like *ung* in German 'Jung'
-ian is like 'yen'
ui is like 'way'

FOOTNOTE

You may have noticed that there are no words given for 'Yes', 'No' or 'Please.' This is because there are no direct equivalents. Instead of 'Yes' you could sometimes use *dùi-le*, which really means 'correct'; instead of 'No,' you could sometimes use *bù*, but since this really means 'not' and is generally followed by the verb used in the preceding question, it does tend to sound rather blunt on its own. As for 'Please,' you will hear Chinese people using either *qǐng* followed by a verb, but this literally means 'I invite you to. . .' and cannot be used, for example, when buying things in shops.

12

Did You Know?

'Primal forces — Yin and Yang'

Concepts of *yin* and *yang*

For thousands of years, Chinese cosmology has divided up the universe into the complementary aspects of things, the two primal forces or modes of creation – *yin* and *yang*. (These terms will be well-known to those who have read the classic of divination, the *Yi Jing*, or *Book of Changes*.)

Although they represent the polar aspects of things, however, as one force reaches its extreme, it produces its opposite and thus there is a never-ending cycle, both on the physical and metaphysical planes. *Yin* corresponds to earth, moon, female, cold, dark, etc., whereas *yang* corresponds to heaven, sun, male, heat, brightness, etc. As *yin* and *yang* alternate, so night is followed by day, the seasons rotate, and so on. This very basic principle of the balance of forces is embedded in Chinese thought.

Feng Shui

Habitually (and inaccurately) translated as 'geomancy', this term literally means 'wind and water', and refers to the traditional Chinese belief that there are influences in the natural environment which affect people's fortunes. Every hill, field and body of water is thought to be able to influence such things as the siting of graves, temples, homes and (especially these days) offices.

In theory, *feng shui* has been banned in the PRC as 'superstition', but in Taiwan and Hong Kong, and in many overseas Chinese communities, it is still very much a part of life.

Since the calculations and esoteric knowledge needed for choosing an auspicious site are very complex, families or organizations will call in an expert geomancer, often at considerable expense, and consult him before any decisions are made. He will use a special kind of compass to work out the most propitious spots, and in most cases this means siting the grave or house or office in such a position that it will bring good fortune to the family or organization involved. It is not unknown, however, for the site to be chosen specifically in order to ruin the *feng shui* of someone else's site, and this has sometimes proved a useful way of carrying on feuds between families or clans.

Chinese 'Horoscopes'

There are two sets of symbols in China – the 10 Heavenly Stems and the 12 Earthly Branches – which, when combined together, have traditionally been used to designate years, months and days. Associated with the 12 Earthly Branches are the names of 12 animals, and a Chinese person will always be able to tell you which animal he 'belongs' to, i.e. which animal is associated with the year in which he was born. The order is: Rat, Ox, Tiger, Hare, Dragon, Snake, Horse, Sheep (or Goat), Monkey, Cock, Dog and Pig. In this system, 1995 is the year of the Pig (as 2007 will be), and 1996 will be the year of the Rat (and so will 2008) and so on.